MARKING SUCCESS

MARKING SUCCESS

A guide to evaluation for teachers of English

Neil Graham/Jerry George

Pembroke Publishers Limited

© 1992 Pembroke Publishers
538 Hood Road
Markham, Ontario L3R 3K9

Canadian Cataloguing in Publication Data

Graham, Neil
  Marking success: a guide to evaluation for
teachers of English

Includes bibliographical references.
ISBN 0-921217-85-4

1. Language arts (Secondary). 2. English language —
Study and teaching (Secondary). I. George, Jerry.
II. Title.

LB1631.G72 1992   428'.0071'2   C92-094771-9

Editor: Joanne Close
Design: John Zehethofer
Cover Illustration: Constantine Zottas
Typesetting: Jay Tee Graphics Ltd.

This book was produced with the generous assistance of the government of Ontario through the Ministry of Culture and Communications.

Printed and bound in Canada
9 8 7 6 5 4 3 2 1

Contents

Introduction

The village all declar'd how much he knew;
'Twas certain he could write and cipher too:
Lands he could measure, terms and tides presage,
And even the story ran that he could gauge:
In arguing, too, the parson own'd his skill,
For, even though vanquish'd he could argue still;
While words of learned length and thundering sound
Amazed the gazing rustics rang'd around;
And still they gaz'd and still the wonder grew,
That one small head could carry all he knew.

Oliver Goldsmith, "The Village Master"
from *The Deserted Village*

The days of the old-fashioned schoolmaster, in complete control of students and of knowledge, have long passed, but many of the qualities commonly attributed to this stereotype linger on in public perception. Many people wistfully look back to a time when they think educators knew their roles and how they were to be fulfilled. These same people picture rows of children busily reading in turn, doing arithmetic exercises, and generally preparing for life and the world of work. And part of this readiness, they think, is that periodically students must undergo tests and examinations in order to demonstrate their knowledge.

  This view of education, if it ever was valid, is not adequate for today's world. The sheer quantity of information and the technology required to accommodate its storage, retrieval, and transmission requires a drastic shift in the concept of education.

Today's students need to know how to access and process information, and how to work both independently and cooperatively. Today's teachers have to know how to arrange their classrooms so that students can practise the skills and acquire the attitudes they need in order to flourish in today's and tomorrow's world. This student-centered interactive curriculum requires a concurrent shift in how we think about evaluation and how we use it. The purpose of this book is to demonstrate the processes of evaluation in a student-centered interactive curriculum and to offer teachers and students a range of evaluation approaches.

Taking Stock

> Come, come, and sit you down; you shall not budge;
> You go not till I set you up a glass
> Where you may see the inmost part of you.
>
> Shakespeare, "Hamlet"

An interesting way for you to look at the contents of this book is to start with a quick look at your own situation and that of your school in terms of evaluation approaches. The page that follows will give you an idea of your own and your school's situation.

By circling the number that most closely describes your practice or school climate, you'll get an idea of your position with respect to evaluation practices. This diagnostic instrument could also form the basis for staff discussion and planning.

ASSESSMENT AND EVALUATION PRACTICES

Traditional Practices	1	2	3	4	5	Current Trends
Focus on end of unit, term course tests, and exams	1	2	3	4	5	Focus on ongoing assessment and evaluation
Teacher-designed strategies	1	2	3	4	5	Students often involved in planning and designing
Teacher as sole evaluator	1	2	3	4	5	Varied evaluators — teacher, self, peer, and others
Use of common instruments and strategies for everyone	1	2	3	4	5	Variation as appropriate to accommodate learning styles
Evaluation focused on proving knowledge of content	1	2	3	4	5	Evaluation focused on application, evaluation, and innovative adaptation of knowledge
Specific objectives and criteria not evident in instruments and procedures	1	2	3	4	5	Specific objectives and criteria articulated
Evaluation results used as judgments of student achievement	1	2	3	4	5	Evaluation results also used to change objectives, program, or strategies

CHAPTER ONE

The Impact of Changing Goals of Education

The emphasis on the processes of learning in today's classroom affects the role of the teacher, the organization of the classroom, and the activities that take place there. The teacher has become less an arbiter of knowledge and more a guide, helping students to access and manage information. The classroom is flexibly organized to enable students to be actively engaged in their learning through planning, carrying out, and evaluating activities, individually and in groups. To ensure that students learn how to function independently in all work situations, curricula often mandate a carefully planned independent study component with as much focus on the processes involved as on the products produced.

Such a learner-centered curriculum has broad implications for everyone involved in education. The key implications for each group involved are listed below.

For students it means:

- having greater involvement in and responsibility for their own learning, including assessment and evaluation;
- focusing on continuous and steady effort. Process-based learning requires participation. Nonperforming and/or nonattending students will be unable to rescue themselves by a "one-shot" product or effort, such as a final examination or essay;
- being aware that their assessment and evaluation involves behavioral objectives, as well as those of knowledge and skills;

- accepting a wider range of learning and evaluation experiences, including individual and group learning, independent learning, and peer- and self-assessment and evaluation.

For teachers it means:

- paying careful attention to unit planning to measure the integral connection and interaction between objectives and teaching/learning approaches, and assessment and evaluation strategies;
- collaborating with other teachers, both in designing programs and in assessing and evaluating students;
- making frequent use of ongoing diagnostic and formative assessment and evaluation to determine individual student needs and progress, as well as to set and modify objectives and devise appropriate teaching/learning approaches;
- involving students in the learning process—setting objectives (both short- and long-term), devising teaching/learning approaches, and establishing assessment and evaluation criteria to measure progress and outcomes;
- teaching assessment and evaluation as thinking skills through integrating peer- and self-assessment and evaluation into the program;
- applying a broad range of objectives that accommodate different learning styles in order to evaluate students' success.

For department heads and principals it means:

- re-examining and revising school evaluation policies to reflect the new integrated and collaborative nature of student evaluation and the role of traditional tests and examinations;
- re-evaluating existing test or examination exemption policies in view of the focus on evaluation as supportive rather than punitive in nature;
- assessing the quality of standardized tests being used in the school or system, and the impact of such a test or tests on the curriculum;
- planning to use some professional development time to encourage teachers to review programs, share material, and

provide time to design and/or evaluate assessment instruments, and to practise their student assessment and evaluation skills collaboratively.

For parents and the public it means:

- becoming aware that, in order to prepare students to be successful, schools are no longer limiting evaluation to the mastery of a narrow range of subject content and academic skills often referred to as "the basics." In addition, a broader evaluation focus is employed that includes behavioral elements, as well as a wide variety of thinking and communication skills that promote success in today's and tomorrow's world;
- realizing that students are being evaluated on the basis of their effort and accomplishment, both individually and in groups;
- understanding that students are being evaluated largely for their success in meeting specific program objectives and identified criteria related to self-improvement, rather than comparing them with one another;
- understanding that paper and pencil tests are no longer the sole or even major means of evaluating student success. The emphasis is on the evaluation of students' performances when they are asked to apply their learning to meaningful situations.

The Impact of Changing Goals on the Teaching of English

In the English classroom, the teaching of literature (used here in the larger sense of varieties of print, oral, and visual "text") has always aimed for the development of appreciation. Traditionally, this was accomplished through close textual analysis (comprehension), along with the analysis of the interpretation of various expert critics of a particular work. Evaluation of student success with this "lit-crit" approach often led students to commercially produced "Notes" that indicated what was to be "appreciated" about a particular work. Students then used these notes as a basis to demonstrate appreciation in essays and on tests and examinations, supporting their note-inspired thoughts with examples and details from the work.

The current approach to teaching literature focuses more on personal response; that is, students' think through their own response to what they are engaged in by applying their own experience and judgment to the work. Thus, instead of giving students an interpretation of a work or referring them to the critics, teachers encourage students to respond individually and in groups to the texts with which they work, and to trust their own judgments as valid milestones on the road to appreciation.

Once the shift is made to a personal response-based approach to literature, it quickly becomes apparent that traditional assessment and evaluation approaches are no longer adequate or appropriate. Robert Probst, in *Response and Analysis: Teaching Literature in Junior and Senior High School*, describes the needed shift in emphasis in assessment and evaluation.

> One frequent objection to response-based literature . . . is that it would make testing difficult or impossible. Clearly it is difficult to test, in any traditional sense, the students' unique and changing interactions with the literature. To test someone's reading of a literary work we would have to know her better than she is likely to know herself. We would have to understand the interplay of events in her life—the works she has read, the people she has met, and her thoughts and feelings about these experiences. Without that knowledge and insight, we would be unqualified to judge her interaction with the work.
>
> We can judge some of it, of course. . . . But the more subtle and more essential matters are not so manageable. Questions of values and beliefs, and judgements about the significance of a literary work for the student, only the student herself can decide. . . . . But responsibility for evaluation must lie primarily with the student, since she is the only one with access to the necessary information.
>
> Robert Probst, *Response and Analysis: Teaching Literature in Junior and Senior High School*, Boynton-Cook (1988: 222-3)

The teaching of writing has also shifted its focus, based on research findings that indicate that attention to the process produces a better product. The development and use of writing folders is a major indication of the value that is now placed on writing as a process.

Folders create a writer's workshop approach to writing, with students working interactively, writing for various purposes and audiences, experimenting with their writing, selecting pieces to revise, edit, and polish, and assessing and evaluating their own and others' work. The accumulation of writing in the folders provides information on important processes and on final products, as well as on progress and achievement.

In *Teaching and Assessing Writing*, Edward M. White points out the importance of evaluation in the writing process.

> An even more compelling reason for writing teachers to consider an understanding of evaluation an indispensable part of their professional development concerns the strange paradox of revision: professional writers revise constantly, while naive and untrained writers, whose need for revision is much more severe, almost never revise. . . . Instructors spend endless hours meticulously marking papers in the belief that grading papers is the same as teaching writing. . . . When we look at this situation, in all its busy futility, the pressing need for teacher sophistication in evaluation becomes inescapable. Even serious students fail to revise, by and large, because they do not know how to evaluate their writing. . . . When papers or drafts are turned in, teachers will prepare, or work with the class to prepare, a scoring guide . . . such a guide allows students to be part of the grading and responding process for one another's papers as well . . . the openness of such a process encourages revision, since students learn to see the differences between the various qualities of writing and hence can begin to see what can be done to improve their work.
>
> Edward M. White, *Teaching and Assessing Writing*, Jossey-Bass Publishers (1988: 6)

In today's English classroom, then, students and teachers are engaged in assessing and evaluating processes continuously in both reading and writing programs. For students, learning how to evaluate their work becomes an important and integral part of the curriculum. The critical thinking skills at the heart of evaluation are discussed, modeled, and taught. Students must learn to judge their own work to truly become independent learners — the goal of today's education.

The Distinction between Assessment and Evaluation

Assessment and evaluation are two terms that are often used interchangeably. However, a valid distinction can and should be made. Assessment is the collection of data — test results, pieces of writing, observational checklists, anecdotal reports, etc. — that forms the basis of the evaluation or judgment of student achievement.

The Distinction among Diagnostic, Formative, and Summative Assessment and Evaluation

Depending on their purpose, both assessment and evaluation can be used for diagnostic, formative, or summative purposes. Diagnostic refers to assessing and evaluating through the gathering of data and the making of judgments with regard to a student's background — his/her knowledge, experience, capabilities, dispositions, and so on. Formative is concerned with assessing and judging the student's ongoing progress in the program — is the student succeeding? Should adjustments be made in program content or teaching strategies? Summative refers to collecting data and making judgments at the end of a unit or course — to what extent has the student accomplished the objectives of the unit or course?

Teachers have always used all three types of assessment or evaluation in formal and informal situations. However, as students move up through the grades, and particularly at the secondary level, summative evaluation takes over as the major, and sometimes only, focus. When the emphasis is on covering the curriculum and on measuring students' success with the curriculum, teachers have less time to pay to diagnostic and formative assessment and evaluation.

However, the new curricular emphasis on the processes of learning and on the importance of teaching assessment and evaluation as thinking skills requires greater balance among all three types of assessment. As well, research into learning indicates that attention to ongoing diagnostic and formative assessment and evaluation ultimately improves performance and outcomes.

CHAPTER TWO

Principles of Student Assessment and Evaluation

Three key principles underlie all sound approaches to the assessment and evaluation of student achievement.

1. Sound assessment and evaluation derive from stated objectives and are consistent with the teaching/learning strategies employed to achieve those objectives.
2. Sound assessment and evaluation are appropriate for the concepts being taught and the students being evaluated.
3. Sound assessment and evaluation are based on specified criteria.

There should be a direct and obvious link in the three curriculum elements.

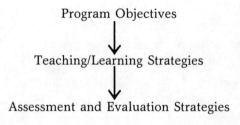

Program Objectives

Teaching/Learning Strategies

Assessment and Evaluation Strategies

These three key principles should not only be kept in mind by the teacher; they should be understood, discussed, and internalized by the students. In order to develop their thinking skills, students should always understand the purposes of an activity. When they ask, "What are we really trying to do?", they are forced to focus on objectives. When they know what the purposes are, they will be better able to select the most appropriate means to determine how they are progressing. As well, they will be better able to know when they have finally finished and what they have achieved. Students should be given time to discuss and clarify the criteria by which their achievements will be judged — by themselves, by their peers, and by the teacher.

1. *Principle One: Sound assessment and evaluation derive from stated objectives and are consistent with the teaching/learning strategies employed to achieve those objectives.*

As Kenneth and Yetta Goodman and Wendy Hood so aptly put it in their book *The Whole Language Evaluation Book* (Heinemann, 1989), "Learning without objectives is like sailing without a compass. You may eventually get somewhere but you won't know where you are when you get there."

Successful learning begins with a clear idea of direction and intended outcomes. Students who are aware of where they are starting from, where they are going, and how they are going to get there are more likely to arrive at their intended goal. Specified curriculum and program objectives help determine appropriate starting points, teaching/learning strategies, and assessment and evaluation techniques. Creating such continuity in the learning process ensures effective learning. Successful learning also begins when learners are involved in their learning, and that means being involved in the articulation and selection of learning objectives. Only when learners are involved in setting learning goals does learning become something that they are motivated to do, rather than something that is done to them.

Assessment and evaluation focus on learning outcomes. These learning outcomes are the objectives of any program. For example, a diagnostic objective would be that "Students would be able to diagnose their own reading level." An important formative objective in teaching writing would be that "Students will gain experience in reading one another's writing in progress and making helpful suggestions for improvement" or "Students will gain experience in designing criteria sheets that produce good feedback from other students on their writing in progress". Ultimately such formative objectives turn into summative objectives when it is deemed necessary to evaluate and measure how well the students have developed the ability to do these things. For example, "Students will become proficient in designing formative criteria sheets".

The following is a partial list of verbs that cover a variety of diagnostic, formative, and summative learning objectives. Students will:

achieve	encourage	identify	master
acquire	experience	improve	model
appreciate	follow	increase	prepare
deepen	foster	know	promote
demonstrate	gain	manipulate	understand
develop			

It is the particular combination of objectives within each program or unit of study that determines the teaching/learning strategies and assessment and evaluation techniques.

The following form provides simple ways to increase students' awareness of the importance of learning objectives and for establishing formative objectives. Notice that on the second part of the form, the task is turned over to the student. A completed form has been included to demonstrate the approach.

SETTING GOALS

YOUR GOAL

_____ *Sharon Chenier* _____ during the next month
(Student's Name)

you should try to *improve your group skills*
_____
_____
_____

I will know that you are working on this goal whenever I see you:

1. *in attendance and working with your group*
2. *contributing to group discussion*
3. *completing tasks with the group*

MY GOAL

I _____ *Sharon* _____ will try to
work with my group regularly. I will try to be more helpful.
_____
_____
_____

You will know that I am working on this goal whenever you see me:

1. *discussing topics with my group*
2. *listening to other members when they talk*
3. *helping the group complete assignments*

SETTING GOALS

YOUR GOAL

_____ during the next month
(Student's Name)

you should try to _____

_____

_____

_____

I will know that you are working on this goal whenever I see you:

1. _____
2. _____
3. _____

MY GOAL

I _____ will try to

_____

_____

_____

_____

You will know that I am working on this goal whenever you see me:

1. _____
2. _____
3. _____

2. *Principle two: Sound assessment and evaluation strategies are appropriate for the concepts being taught and the students being evaluated.*

When you break out of the traditional mold of written assessment and evaluation, you begin to see that the range of assessment and evaluation strategies is vast. More teachers and students are experimenting with discussion and observation as a means of assessing and evaluating the ongoing processes of learning. The key lies in developing strategies and instruments that demonstrate progress over time, and that permit students to demonstrate their learning orally, visually, and in written form, individually and in groups.

The following pages demonstrate approaches that break out of the traditional mold of written assessment and evaluation. The first is a test and examination template that allows students to demonstrate their learning in a variety of ways. The second and third are based on the target symbol as a method of tracking progress and achievement over time.

TEST AND EXAMINATION TEMPLATE FOR ENGLISH

Topic: Romeo and Juliet

Time	Task
Time	*Task*
05 min.	1. For the past few weeks, you have been exploring Shakespeare's play, ROMEO AND JULIET. For the purposes of this final examination, you will focus on Act III, scene v. 11. As you will recall, this is the scene in which Capulet gets angry at his daughter Juliet for not wishing to marry Paris.
20 min.	2. Reread this scene. As you read, focus particularly on the changes in Juliet's responses to the other members of her family throughout the scene. To help you concentrate on this progression, Juliet's words have been printed in bold-face type. (Option: You may wish to view the scene on VCR or listen to a professional record. These are also available for your use.)
30 min.	3. Summarize the scene by either writing on paper or dictating into a tape-recorder.
40 min.	4. Describe the scene by either writing on paper or dictating into a tape-recorder any thoughts, feelings, memories, or associations that came to you while you were reading or viewing or listening to it.
40-80 min.	5. Select one of the following talk situations that is comfortable for you and the group: interior individual reflection, exterior talk in pairs, triads, small groups, or large groups. Then, working alone or with others, consider both your summary of the scene and the personal reflections generated by them as doorways to the meaning of the changes in Juliet in this scene.

40-80 min.   6. As the final stage in this examination, you will be required to interpret the meaning you have discovered by generating an outcome. Once again, you may work in familiar talk situations to share your work in progress. You may wish to use the following ideas and steps as a guide.

Initial Response This may be oral, visual, or written — please keep this first version.

Revision or Peer Conferencing If reading your writing aloud to someone else or sharing your materials reveals that what you want to convey isn't what the other person hears or sees, then you may wish to revise your material.

Second or Final Response Prepare a more polished version of your response.
N.B. You may repeat these steps and polish your work until the allotted time comes to an end. Develop a criteria checklist for evaluating your work.

Adapted from *Senior English OAIP: Promoting Learning through Assessment*, Ontario Ministry of Education, 1992.

The Target Symbol

Many schools are beginning to adopt the target symbol to visually represent student progress and achievement. Once the objective has been determined, the criteria for assessing attainment of the objective are agreed upon by both student and teacher, and entries are periodically made on the target. For example, a student may have as an objective the improvement of work and study habits. Some criteria that could be used to evaluate whether there has been improvement could be listed and numbered, for example:

1. perseverance in task completion
2. seeking help when needed
3. meeting timelines.

With this method, the students' best mark, that is, the mark closest to the bull's eye is the mark that counts when a summative judgment is to be made about his/her progress and success.

The following bull's eye writing checklist and oral language checklist could be completed by the teacher, preferably in consultation with the student or students involved. They should agree on the indicators for each criterion. For example, indicators for attitude might include a willingness to use topics from personal experience, a willingness to research topics, and so on. Checkmarks and symbols could be entered on the targets with the purpose of getting to the bull's eye. For each checklist, a completed version prefaces the blank checklist to illustrate its application.

SPEAKING CHECKLIST

Student's Name: _____ *Anna Lee* _____ Class: _____ *7B* _____

Unit/Term: _____ *January-June* _____

Select ONE or TWO indicators for each criterion.

Activity/Date	Record of Observations						Evaluation Targets
	P	*P*	*S*	*P*	*P*	*S*	3 / 2 / 1 / 0
Observer	*Self, Peer, Teacher*						
1. *Attitude*							
a *willingness*	2	3	3	3	3	3	
b *describing*	2	2	2	2	3	3	
2. *Content*							
a *on topic*	1	2	1	3	3	3	
b *judgment*	3	3	3	3	2	3	
3. *Organization*							
a *initial*	3	3	3	3	2	3	
b *sequential*	3	3	3	3	3	3	
4. *Expression*							
a *body language*	2	1	1	2	1	2	3 / 2 / 1 / 0
b *tone*	2	2	2	2	2	2	
5. *Role play*							
a *assuming*	3	3	3	2	2	3	
b *sustaining*	3	2	3	3	3	3	

Comments: *You're right on target in all areas of speaking, except for expression. That will come with practice. Next term, let's use different indicators, except for expression, and challenge you!*

Adapted from *Basic English OAIP: Assessment Strategies and Materials*, Ontario Ministry of Education, 1990.

SPEAKING CHECKLIST

Student's Name: _____ Class: _____

Unit/Term: _____

Select ONE or TWO indicators for each criterion:

	Record of Observations						Evaluation Targets
Activity/Date							(3 2 1 0)
Observer							
1. _____ a _____ b _____							(3 2 1 0)
2. _____ a _____ b _____							(3 2 1 0)
3. _____ a _____ b _____							(3 2 1 0)
4. _____ a _____ b _____							(3 2 1 0)
5. _____ a _____ b _____							(3 2 1 0)

Comments: _____
_____
_____

Adapted from *Basic English OAIP, Assessment Strategies and Materials*, Ontario Ministry of Education, 1990.

ORAL LANGUAGE CHECKLIST

Student's Name: _____ *Carlo Corsetti* _____ Class: _____ *12 G* _____

Unit/Term: _____ *September–December* _____

This checklist enables you to combine criteria from small group learning, speaking, and listening.

Activity/Date	Record of Observations						Evaluation Targets
	S	*T*	*P*	*P*	*S*	*T*	
Observer	*Self, Peer, Teacher*						
Small Group Learning 1. *Discussing*							
a *questioning*	1	2	1		2	2	
b *exploring*	1	1	2		2	2	
2. *Involvement*				*Absent for this activity*			
a *sharing*	2	3	2		3	3	
b *taking risks*	2	3	3		3	3	
Speaking and/or Listening 1. *Speaking*							
a *willingness*	2	3	3		3	3	
b *participation*	2	2	3		3	3	
2. *Listening*							
a *evaluating*	0	0	0		1	2	
b *understanding*	1	0	1		1	2	

Comments: *You're making significant progress in all areas. You need to focus on your listening skills; specifically evaluation, where you were initially ''off target''.*

Adapted from *Basic English OAIP: Assessment Strategies and Materials*, Ontario Ministry of Education, 1990.

ORAL LANGUAGE CHECKLIST

Student's Name: _____ Class: _____

Unit/Term: _____

This checklist enables you to combine criteria from small group learning, speaking, and listening.

	Record of Observations						Evaluation Targets
Activity/Date							③ 3 2 1 0
Observer							
Small Group Learning 1._____ a _____ b _____							③ 3 2 1 0
2._____ a _____ b _____							③ 3 2 1 0
Speaking and/or Listening 1._____ a _____ b _____							③ 3 2 1 0
2._____ a _____ b _____							③ 3 2 1 0

Comments: _____

_____

_____

_____

Adapted from *Basic English OAIP: Assessment Strategies and Materials*, Ontario Ministry of Education, 1990.

3. Principle three: Sound assessment and evaluation are based on specific and specified criteria.

> One can read and interpret various texts in various ways, indeed in various ways simultaneously. Indeed the prevailing view is that we must read and interpret in some multiple way if literary meaning is to be extracted from a text.
>
> Jerome Brunner, *Actual Minds, Possible Worlds*

The personal response emphasis to material studied in the English classroom requires careful consideration of assessment and evaluation criteria. The personal, subjective response to literature is obviously highly individualized and creative. The "creative work" that used to be somewhat on the periphery of English has now become the central focus. Students are invited to deepen their response to material by responding to it in a wide variety of ways and by using a variety of media. The response journal and oral group discussion are at the heart of this approach. The "give three examples of" and "explain the significance of" approaches have metamorphosed into such questions as the one that follows.

Which of the two characters do you think would get along best

1. in a marriage? Why?
2. on a camping trip? Why?
3. sharing an apartment? Why?

With such an approach, students must have a clear idea of the criteria to be considered when engaged in assessing and evaluating. You saw, for example, the importance of articulated criteria in the target symbol instructions on the previous pages.

Applying these Principles to the Traditional Test and Examination

Many people consider the terms "test" and "examination" to be virtually synonymous, with the former thought of as a mini-version of the latter. On the other hand, some find it useful to consider a test — written or oral — as a check or control of content and knowledge, and an examination as the application of that knowledge to a novel situation. Whatever the case, both tests and examinations continue to be an important reality in schools and their design deserves careful consideration.

However, today's curriculum demands that we take a close look at the traditional procedures and practices that are associated with testing and examining. With an emphasis on process and collaboration, it appears to make little sense to examine students by putting them in a "two hours in the gym" environment and isolating them from one another. Many jurisdictions are experimenting with test and examination procedures that permit process and collaboration, as you saw in the example of the group examination on Romeo and Juliet. Whatever the conditions for conducting the test or examination, one factor does remain constant, and that is the question(s) asked.

Three Criteria for Good Test and Examination Questions

Questions on tests and examinations should be framed so that they are relevant, clear, and specific. They should not be "fishing expeditions" to simply see what the students might generate. The expected answer to questions should be outlined by the person setting the questions. Teachers should discuss their questions and expected answers with colleagues for reaction in terms of these three criteria.

Relevance

Is the question relevant to the students and to the course of study? Personal response questions will elicit much more information from students at a deeper level than those that are more traditionally academic and objective. Consider, for example, the increased level of interest likely to be generated as you progress through the following questions.

1. Write a character sketch of _____ in _____.
2. Select a character you admire in _____ and write a character sketch of him/her.
3. Select a character you feel would make a good or bad mother, father, brother, sister, marriage partner, and so on (the list could be

extended depending on the work in question).

(a) What advice would you give ＿＿＿＿ at the end of the story/play/film?

(b) How would you persuade him/her to act differently?

Clarity

The prime requirement of a good question or assignment is clarity, whether it asks for an extended response in the form of an essay or a demonstration. Make sure that students are familiar with the key directive words — usually the verbs — in any question or assignment. In some schools, the development of a common understanding of important directive verbs is a cross-subject activity. Students should be aware of the precise meanings of such verbs as state, explain, discuss, describe, illustrate, list, trace, outline, compare, contrast, analyze, and so on. These verbs are defined on pages 91-93.

Students should also be aware of the thinking levels that certain verbs trigger. The following are considered typical "higher" thinking-level verbs:

agree	defend	paraphrase
analyze	distinguish	predict
argue	evaluate	propose
assess	explore	prove
compare	generalize	recommend
conclude	interpret	suggest
contrast	judge	summarize
criticize	justify	suppose
		synthesize

Specificity

In designing questions and assignments, teachers should strike a balance between giving students too much (organizing their thinking for them) and too little (leaving them open to disorganization).

The level of specificity in questions and assignments should differ between grades. Questions and assignments in a younger

36

division can be more directive and more specific in order to assist students to organize their response; for older students, such elements as organization and format are important aspects of what is being measured, so the level of specificity should decrease.

Criteria and the Writing Process

> Scales, criteria and specific questions that students apply to their own and other's writing also have a powerful effect on enhancing quality. Through using the criteria systematically, students appear to internalize them and bring to bear in generating new material even when they don't have the criteria in front of them.
>
> George Hillocks, Jr., "What Works in Teaching Composition: A Meta-analysis of Experimental Treatment Studies"

Just as an awareness of audience improves writing, so too does an awareness of the criteria by which the writing is to be judged. Students need to write knowing what criteria will eventually be applied to their work. They need to know whether it is the overall impression that will be emphasized or some particular set of criteria or even one criterion (e.g. unity or organization) that they are to focus on and practise until it is internalized. Quality of work is lowered when students write with one set of assumptions in mind and their work is evaluated based on another.

Another reason that criteria are important in today's classroom is that while teachers have always been comfortable with informal discussion and observation as a means of assessment and evaluation, today an increasing number of teachers are also using formal discussion (in the form of an interview) and formal observation as methods of evaluation. The key to sound formal discussion and observation as evaluation techniques lies in the use of the well-designed checklist.

The following checklists demonstrate qualities of a well-designed checklist — criteria are clearly articulated, and the actual worth of each criterion varies according to its importance.

EVALUATION OF PRESENTATION

Title of Presentation: _____

Presenter(s): _____

Date: _____

	Inadequate	Marginally Adequate	Adequate	Very Good	Superior
Content					
Clarity of purpose (thesis)	1	2	3	4	5
Organization of material	1	2	3	4	5
Sufficient supporting information	1	2	3	4	5
Other perspectives dealt with	1	2	3	4	5
Presentation					
Vocal impact	1	2	3	4	5
Appropriate mannerisms (body language)	1	2	3	4	5
Appropriate language	1	2	3	4	5

Overall Impression

Overall Evaluation (circle one of the following):

Superior   Very Good   Adequate
    Marginally Acceptable   Inadequate

Mark: _____
   40

SCORING SHEET FOR INDIVIDUAL STORIES

Student's Name: _____

Title: _____

Date: _____

Grading Criteria
Circle One

Overall Achievement
of Purpose   1   2   3   4

                   (not at all achieved)   (fully achieved)

Structure   1   2   3   4

                   (no single focus or order) (unified and well ordered)

Development
(details, specifics)   1   2   3   4

                   (very little   (fully fleshed with
                   relevant detail)   appropriate detail)

Style   1   2   3   4

                   (general and vague,   (vivid, varied
                   limited vocabulary,   vocabulary and
                   little sentence   sentence structure,
                   variety, choppy)   smooth flowing)

Surface features
(spelling, punctua-
tion, etc.)   1   2   3   4

                   (many errors)   (almost no errors)

Commitment   1   2   3   4

(commitment may be doubled or tripled in value since it represents the process)

Bonus   2   4   6   8

(student is attempting something new and difficult)

Total Grade $\dfrac{\text{Sum of Circled Numbers}}{\text{Total Possible Score}} \times 100$
(as Percent)

Adapted from *Senior English OAIP: Assessing Writing*, Ontario Ministry of Education, 1992.

CHAPTER THREE

The Role of Diagnostic Assessment and Evaluation

For the roses
Had the look of flowers that are looked at.

T. S. Eliot, "Four Quartets"

Diagnostic assessment and evaluation are crucial if students are to be involved in their learning. It indicates their knowledge, motivational, and interest levels. Teachers diagnose in order to make adjustments to the planned program so that students' needs, both as individuals and members of a group, can be better accommodated. Teachers should also instruct students on how to engage in self-diagnosis as a natural part of any learning process. In this way both the teacher and the students can determine their needs at the outset of any undertaking. Without this initial diagnosis, the program remains something that is done to the students, rather than something they do themselves; its pace and direction remains arbitrary and its learning strategies untuned to individual learning styles and needs.

Diagnostic assessment tools such as those on the following pages can reveal a lot about the interests, confidence levels, and learning needs of students. The first is a target symbol. A completed self-assessment is included to demonstrate its uses. The next three are checklists. The fifth, the crest or ensign, is a diagnostic tool that appeals to students because it accommodates different learning styles. The last instrument asks students to complete sentence openers to help them reflect on their beliefs about themselves. All of these instruments can be used as they are or adapted by you and your students to suit your particular diagnostic needs.

Examining the results of any of these assessment instruments will help you determine where to begin with your program and what skills to emphasize. The checklists can also be used as a basis for discussion and as starting points for journal entries. The survey of attitudes toward writing can be completed early in the year or term by the student so that growth goals may be established and an appropriate program planned. The crest or ensign diagnostic tool is also finding favor with teachers and students. Early in the year, you might ask students to design a crest that would tell others something about themselves. The crest can also be adapted and applied to characters in literature or history, both for formative assessment and summative evaluation purposes. Instead of drawing, students could use calligraphy, or pictures of symbols cut from newspapers or magazines.

These diagnostic instruments should be kept for future reference. Depending on how you use them, you may wish to file them away for future comparative reference, or students could file them in the appropriate folder or file. Whatever the case, students should have an opportunity to review the instruments periodically so that growth and change can be recognized. These files could also become part of the student's achievement profile.

SELF-ASSESSMENT TARGET: WORK AND STUDY HABITS

Name: _____   Date: _____

Assess yourself in each of the work and study habits shown on the target below.

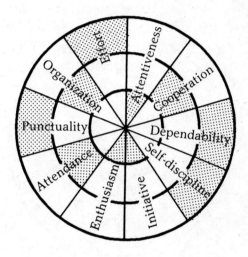

Areas of Strength: *Enthusiasm, initiative, attentiveness*

Areas of Need: *Punctuality, effort, self discipline, dependability*

From *Basic English OAIP: Assessment Strategies and Materials*, Ontario Ministry of Education, 1990.

SELF-ASSESSMENT TARGET

Name: _____ Date: _____

Assess yourself in each of the work and study habits shown on the target below.

Areas of Strength: _____

Areas of Need: _____

From *Basic English OAIP: Assessment Strategies and Materials*, Ontario Ministry of Education, 1990.

WRITING ATTITUDE SURVEY

Circle the number that best describes your attitude toward writing.

1 = Strongly agree   2 = Agree   3 = Uncertain
4 = Disagree   5 = Strongly disagree

1. I avoid writing.   1 2 3 4 5
2. I am not afraid of having my writing evaluated.   1 2 3 4 5
3. I look forward to writing down my ideas.   1 2 3 4 5
4. I am afraid of writing essays when I know they will be evaluated.   1 2 3 4 5
5. Taking a composition course is a very frightening experience.   1 2 3 4 5
6. Handing in a composition makes me feel good.   1 2 3 4 5
7. My mind seems to go blank when I start to work on a composition.   1 2 3 4 5
8. Expressing ideas through writing seems to be a waste of time.   1 2 3 4 5
9. I would like to submit my writing to magazines for evaluation and publication.   1 2 3 4 5
10. I like to write down my ideas.   1 2 3 4 5
11. I feel confident in my ability to express my ideas clearly in writing.   1 2 3 4 5
12. I like to have my friends read what I have written.   1 2 3 4 5
13. I'm nervous about writing.   1 2 3 4 5
14. People seem to enjoy what I write.   1 2 3 4 5
15. I enjoy writing.   1 2 3 4 5
16. I never seem to be able to write down my ideas clearly.   1 2 3 4 5
17. Writing is a lot of fun.   1 2 3 4 5
18. I expect to do poorly in composition classes, even before I enter them.   1 2 3 4 5
19. I like seeing my thoughts on paper.   1 2 3 4 5
20. Discussing my writing with others is an enjoyable experience.   1 2 3 4 5
21. I have a terrible time organizing my ideas in a composition course.   1 2 3 4 5
22. When I hand in a composition, I know I'm going to do poorly.   1 2 3 4 5
23. It's easy for me to write a good composition.   1 2 3 4 5
24. I don't think I write as well as most people.   1 2 3 4 5
25. I don't like my compositions to be evaluated.   1 2 3 4 5
26. I'm not good at writing.   1 2 3 4 5

READING SELF-EVALUATION

Name: _____   Class: _____

Date: _____   Teacher: _____

In the program this year, we will be focusing on the objectives listed below. Use the list to indicate (a) how much experience you have had, and (b) how confident you feel about doing each objective.

Scale: 1: none, not at all
       2: a little
       3: quite a lot
       4: very much, very well

Experience   Confidence

1. _____ guess what's going to happen in a story   1. _____

2. _____ state the author's purpose   2. _____

3. _____ find main ideas   3. _____

4. _____ identify cause and effect relationships   4. _____

5. _____ distinguish between fact and opinion   5. _____

6. _____ tell what I think about what I've read   6. _____

7. _____ evaluate the quality of what I've read   7. _____

8. _____ identify themes and agree/disagree with them   8. _____

9. _____ see similarities in other books or stories by the same author   9. _____

10. _____ identify the author's writing style and give examples   10. _____

TRAITS OF EFFECTIVE READERS

Name: _____ Date: _____

This checklist enables you to see some of the characteristics of effective readers. On a scale of 1-5, indicate the characteristics you feel you have as a reader.

Scale:
1 = not at all, never
2 = a little
3 = sometimes, to some extent
4 = often, quite well
5 = always

As a reader, I

_____ choose reading over something else when I have spare time

_____ respond sensitively to literature

_____ recognize literature as a source of ideas, opinions, and information

_____ use literature as a stimulus for personal reflection

_____ appreciate the importance of style in literature

_____ get ideas from books

_____ predict the outcome before I get to the end

_____ write a different story ending that makes sense

_____ see and appreciate the effect of figurative language

_____ recognize connections among ideas, images, and themes

_____ make generalizations from what is read

_____ make inferences from what is read

_____ conclude the messages and morals of a text

_____ analyze texts for literary devices

_____ relate what I read to my own experience

YOUR ENSIGN

Name: _____ Date: _____

An ensign is a symbol that shows others who you are, and how you want to be seen. Follow the instructions below to complete your own ensign.

Your ensign does not have to be a great work of art. What is important is that you keep your personality, goals, and image in mind, and allow them to come through in your work.

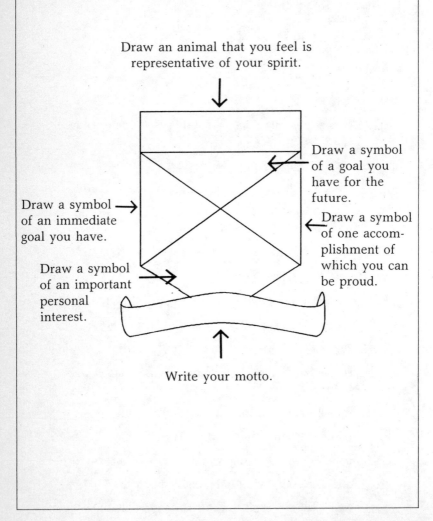

Draw an animal that you feel is representative of your spirit.

Draw a symbol of a goal you have for the future.

Draw a symbol of an immediate goal you have.

Draw a symbol of one accomplishment of which you can be proud.

Draw a symbol of an important personal interest.

Write your motto.

From *Basic English OAIP: Assessment and Strategies*, Ontario Ministry of Education, 1990.

SELF-ASSESSMENT: OPINIONS

Name: _____ Date: _____

Use the following sentence openers to help you reflect on what you believe about yourself.

1. My favorite subject in school is _____

2. Most of my teachers are _____

3. Going to college is _____

4. I hope that I can _____

5. Doing homework is _____

6. I am unhappy when _____

7. I wonder if _____

8. The most important person I know is _____

9. My parents feel that my report cards are _____

10. I hope that I will never have to _____

11. I sometimes get nervous when _____

12. I am happiest when _____

13. The thing I want most out of life is _____

14. The world would be a better place if _____

15. I feel most hurt when _____

16. When I'm happy, _____

17. People are _____

18. Life is _____

19. When I get out of school, I hope to _____

20. If I could be anything in the world, I would want to be

_____

From *Basic English OAIP: Assessment Strategies and Materials*, Ontario Ministry of Education, 1990.

CHAPTER FOUR

The Role of Formative Assessment and Evaluation

Formative assessment and evaluation focuses on the processes of learning and is designed to help students improve as they work toward completion of a task. Formative assessment and evaluation usually takes the form of discussion, comments, or checklists that provide helpful feedback to both teachers and learners about work in progress or about a developing skill.

The following sample instruments illustrate how this type of assessment and evaluation works in practice. Think about involving students in the construction of their own assessment instruments, or have them re-design or modify what you give them. This will help students to focus on what they really need to know about the specific endeavor, develop their thinking skills, and assist them in being more objective about their own learning.

Formative Assessment and Evaluation of Written Work

One of the most powerful assessment tools for formative evaluation in the writing program is the use of peer feedback, either written or oral. In order for the feedback to be effective, the partners need guidance, both in framing the questions they should be asking and in the type of responses they should be giving. Students should be encouraged to form questions that have personal relevance, so that they can get specific feedback to help them improve their work.

On the pages that follow are four examples of formative feedback instruments. The first three focus on feedback during the writing process; the fourth is a learning log, another good strategy for getting students involved in formative evaluation.

The first formative criteria sheet asks for specific feedback on an application, in this case, a job application letter. The second criteria sheet contains examples of the sorts of questions that a writer can pose in a writing conference. The third is a checklist for a reader to give written feedback on a piece of writing in progress. A completed student response has been included to demonstrate the application of the checklist. In all cases, the writer should have a clearer idea of how to improve the piece through further revision based on peer response. These instruments could be adapted and others made from them that are appropriate for specific pieces of writing or for other activities.

These criteria sheets can be used for summative evaluation, if, at some point, you wished to evaluate the students' ability to apply the principles of good formative feedback. Summative marks can be awarded based on the student's ability to give such feedback to another student. Learning log entries can be judged for completion of the number of entries assigned, rather than for their "content."

JOB APPLICATION LETTER CHECKLIST

Name: _____ Date: _____

LETTER	Yes	No
Return address is complete and correct	☐	☐
Inside address is complete and correct	☐	☐
Proper punctuation follows salutation	☐	☐
Spacing and indentation is correct	☐	☐
Reason for writing is stated clearly (in the first paragraph)	☐	☐
Education and relevant courses are stated	☐	☐
Reference is made to résumé	☐	☐
Relevant work experience is stated	☐	☐
Interview is requested	☐	☐
Phone number is given	☐	☐
Language (word choice, tone) is appropriate	☐	☐
Letter is clear and concise	☐	☐
Closing is appropriate	☐	☐
Proper punctuation follows closing	☐	☐
Signature is clear	☐	☐
Name is given under signature, where applicable	☐	☐
Enclosure is indicated	☐	☐
Résumé is enclosed	☐	☐

Checked by: _____

_____

From *Senior English OAIP: Assessing Writing*, Ontario Ministry of Education, 1992.

QUESTIONS FOR A WRITING CONFERENCE

Name: _____ Date: _____

1. How do you feel about my work? What impression does it leave you with?

   _____

   _____

2. I wanted to create an interesting lead. Did I succeed in catching your attention?

   _____

   _____

3. What do you think my main idea/theme is?

   _____

   _____

4. I tried to use the following for effect. Select from the following:

   comparisons/contrasts   irony/humor/satire
   illustrations/examples   images/metaphors/symbols
   anecdotes   parallelism/balance

   _____

   _____

   Can you find them? Are they effective? Are there too many? not enough?

   _____

   _____

5. I was unsure about paragraphing. Can you make suggestions for revising?

   _____

   _____

6. Are there any sentences or places that aren't clear?

   _____

   _____

7. Can you suggest how I might improve . . . ?

   _____

   _____

8. How would you describe the tone/mood of the piece? Do you think it could be improved? How?

   _____

   _____

WRITING CHECKLIST

Name: _____ Date: _____

Comments

1. Have I clearly stated my opinion, my point of view?

    Yes　　　　No

    Underline the sentence or sentences that you think give my opinion.

    I think, though, I would have liked it more "up front!" — in your first paragraph.

2. How convincing is my evidence and support?

    Not very　Somewhat　Very

    Write a 1 in the margin beside what you think is my most important point and 12 beside my least.

    You only gave two samples to support your main point. I think you missed the key one — what did he do in the second act?

3. Do you have any suggestions for more evidence or support?

    See above — look at his actions in Act II.

4. I tried to acknowledge other perspectives and deal with them? How many other opinions did you see?

    1　　　　2　　　　3

    Do you think I left out any important ones? If so, please specify.

    Maybe two — the second one is more implied than stated — put it up front for poor readers like me!

5. Describe how you think my ideas are organized.

    Logically — cause & effect

6. Bracket any sentences that you found hard to read or comprehend.

    See your paper

7. Indicate any mechanical errors by placing the following symbols above the error:

    gr — grammar, p — punctuation,
    sp — spelling

    Not many — what about comma in 3rd sentence, para. 3 — should be a semicolon

8. I tried to use language that would get the reader involved. Please circle four or five words that you think are effective.

    I really liked "mendacity" — a neat word — I didn't know it.

9. Overall, to what extent do you think I have achieved my purpose? Please check one of descriptions below and comment.

    Not convincing　　Somewhat convincing
    Quite convincing　　Totally convincing

    A (little) more evidence and I would be totally (& utterly) convinced! Good work!

WRITING CHECKLIST

Name: _____ Date: _____

Comments

1. Have I clearly stated my opinion, my point of view?
   Yes   No
   Underline the sentence or sentences that you think give my opinion.
2. How convincing is my evidence and support?
   Not very   Somewhat   Very
   Write a 1 in the margin beside what you think is my most important point and 12 beside my least.
3. Do you have any suggestions for more evidence or support?
4. I tried to acknowledge other perspectives and deal with them? How many other opinions did you see?
   1   2   3
   Do you think I left out any important ones? If so, please specify.
5. Describe how you think my ideas are organized.
6. Bracket any sentences that you found hard to read or comprehend.
7. Indicate any mechanical errors by placing the following symbols above the error:
   gr — grammar, p — punctuation,
   sp — spelling
8. I tried to use language that would get the reader involved. Please circle four or five words that you think are effective.
9. Overall, to what extent do you think I have achieved my purpose? Please check one of descriptions below and comment.
   Not convincing   Somewhat convincing
   Quite convincing   Totally convincing

LEARNING LOG ENTRY FORM

Use the following form after a lesson or unit of work. The answers will help both you and your teacher know how well you have learned and what remains to be done.

Name: _____ Date: _____

Teacher: _____

Purpose/Object of Unit or Lesson

_____

_____

1. What I did

_____

_____

_____

_____

2. What I learned

_____

_____

_____

_____

3. What questions I still have

_____

_____

_____

_____

Formative Assessment and Evaluation of Group Work

In order for group work to be effective, formative assessment and evaluation of the process should be built into the task. The following instruments demonstrate how this may be done. Again, as with the previous instruments, if marks are to be given for this activity, they should be awarded for completion of task rather than for the quality of what is said. This encourages honesty, and ensures that summative evaluation does not distort the learning process.

GROUP WORK EVALUATION CHECKLIST

After your group has met, use the following checklist for debriefing to determine how well the group is working and what could be done to make it work better. If you can think of additional points, please add them.

Names: _____

_____

_____

Date: _____ Class: _____

As a group, we	Yes	No	Not Sure
1. knew what we were trying to accomplish			
2. got on task			
3. talked openly and on topic			
4. listened to one another			
5. allowed and encouraged everyone to participate			
6. tried to reach consensus			
7. asked for clarifications as needed			
8. paraphrased one another's point of view			
9.			
10.			

GROUP PARTICIPATION CHECKLIST

Group Members: _____

_____

Date: _____ Class: _____

	Low 1	2	Moderate 3	4	High 5
How satisfied do you feel about the group at this moment?					
How satisfied are you with the amount and quality of your participation in the group?					
How satisfied are you with the leadership provided by members of the group?					
To what extent were your opinions and thoughts asked for and valued in the group?					
How open and free were you to express your own thoughts?					
How clear were your group goals?					
How effective were you in helping your group to reach its goals?					
How committed was the group in facing its problems?					

From *Linking Evaluation with Learning in Science*, The Metropolitan Toronto School Board, 1989.

Formative Assessment and Evaluation of a Student Notebook

Students often need help in keeping an orderly, organized, and therefore useful notebook. A formative assessment checklist such as the one shown here could be kept by the student at the front of his/her notebook. Check the notebook periodically for the items listed. You could also invite the students to alter the list or add items that they think are important and useful to them. Of course, if you plan to summatively evaluate the notebook eventually, the completed checklist can be one of the criteria included in the evaluation.

NOTEBOOK CHECKLIST

Name: _____ Date: _____

Organization	Date	Date	Date	Date
use of tabs, dividers				
ease of access to contents				
visual layout				
use of color, space, design				
creativity				

Comments

_____

_____

_____

_____

Content	Date	Date	Date	Date
dates entered				
neatness				
legibility				
course outline				
objectives				
clarity				
reminders				
cross references				
assignments				

Comments

_____

_____

_____

_____

CHAPTER FIVE

The Role of Summative Assessment and Evaluation

Summative assessment and evaluation occur when students are ready to demonstrate their success with identified curriculum objectives. The assessment instruments are designed to enable teachers and students to make judgments about the value or merit of work accomplished. These judgments are based on specific criteria derived from program objectives. These criteria can be laid out in a checklist, often collaboratively designed by both teacher and students. Involving students in designing checklists increases the likelihood that they will understand and internalize the criteria by which their accomplishments will be judged. Such involvement becomes a powerful teaching strategy.

Summative evaluation is recognized by the awarding of a mark or a grade for objectives met and work accomplished. As you saw in the previous section, formative assessment and evaluation is a process intended to help the student make adjustments when necessary so that the final objectives and the completed work can be more successfully achieved. You also saw in the previous section how summative evaluation can be applied if you wish to evaluate students' success with formative objectives, such as giving appropriate feedback to others for work in progress.

The Issue of Process and Product Assessment and Evaluation

Some educators argue that the process–product controversy is a nonissue. Their position is that since the quality of the product is dependent on the quality of the processes that went into it, evaluating the product alone is sufficient. The evaluation of the process introduces an artificial element in the process that can undermine or distort it. Such educators would argue against the use of an observational checklist to measure the quality of an ongoing group activity; evaluation of process should be on the basis of participation in the activity, with no attempt to rate its quality.

On the other hand, others argue that teaching the skill(s) involved in a process itself is typically more important than the individual product, or more often than not, the process itself is the product. An example of this is a student's ability to conduct an interview or engage in role playing with another student. You will be on safe ground in this issue if you distinguish between using a process as a means to an end or as an end in itself.

Generally, it comes to this. If you are overtly teaching process objectives, that is, stages or elements of process that you want students to become proficient in doing, then you can evaluate process as well as product. The balance between the two depends on the relative weight of the process–product objectives you have articulated. And, although you can make judgments about the quality of the observable phases of a process, these judgments are subjective; you cannot really evaluate the nonobservable phases without reference to the final product.

Students should be aware that attention to process ultimately produces a better product. They should be trained to focus on evaluation of process as well as on the product. Questions such as those that follow will help students focus on the quality of the process as they are working through a task, and on the quality of the product when the task has been completed. They should be encouraged to add other questions as they apply to specific endeavors.

Some strategies for assessing or evaluating process include:

- anecdotal response sheets
- checklists
- response journals and learning logs
- interviews

- conferences
- inventories
- progress or tracking charts
- discussions

The following checklists demonstrate the varying emphases that can be put on the evaluation of process and product.

PROCESS EVALUATION CHECKLIST FOR INDEPENDENT STUDY		
Name: _____ Date: _____		
	Marks	Comments
Logs:		
a) completed		
b) neat and readable		
Attendance and Punctuality:		
Conference Preparation:		
a) outline of progress to date		
b) identification of difficulties		
c) willingness to discuss/adapt		
Conference One:		
Conference Two:		
Conference Three:		
Evidence of Independent Study Skills Learned		
Student demonstrates:		
a) efficient use of time		
b) self-direction		
c) respect for library facilities and procedures		
d) appropriate selection of materials		
e) ability to skim and summarize materials		
f) ability to select a topic		
g) ability to focus topic and develop thesis		
h) ability to distinguish and evaluate primary, secondary, and tertiary sources		
i) ability to use library systems and technologies		

From *Independent Learning,* Ontario Secondary School Teachers' Federation, 1989.

PROCESS AND PRODUCT EVALUATION

Name: _____

Class: _____

Teacher: _____

Hours: _____ Date started: _____ Date completed: _____

Title or description of project: _____

_____

Scale
1 = below average
2 = average
3 = above average
4 = outstanding

Process Evaluation
1. Definition and focus of project   _____
2. Identification of problems and problem-solving
   strategies   _____
3. Logical development of ideas   _____
4. Appropriate use of materials and resources   _____
5. Commitment of time and effort   _____

Product Evaluation
1. Originality and creativity of idea   _____
2. Clarity and focus of presentation   _____
3. Mastery of content   _____
4. Level and sophistication of content   _____
5. Care and attention to detail   _____
6. Organization   _____
7. Originality and variety of presentation   _____
8. Value, interest, impact of product to immediate or
   projected audience   _____

Comments

From *Independent Learning*, Ontario Secondary School Teachers' Federation, 1989.

PRODUCT EVALUATION: ORAL REPORT

Name: _____ Date: _____

Topic: _____

Scale

1 = not at all	4 = to a considerable extent
2 = to a small extent	5 = outstanding, to a large
3 = to some extent	extent

Content

1. There was a clear thesis, stating an opinion   _____
2. Logical and clear reasons supporting the opinion
   were given   _____
3. The presentation was well researched and
   carefully prepared   _____
4. I understood and learned several things from this
   report, including

_____

_____

_____

_____

_____

_____

Presentation

1. The student spoke clearly   _____
2. The student spoke enthusiastically and invited
   questions   _____
3. The student used a variety of techniques
   (overhead projector, blackboard, humor, concrete
   materials, etc.)   _____
4. The student paid close attention to the time limit   _____
5. The student was able to "think on his/her feet
   without constantly referring to notes"   _____

                                           Total: _____

From *Independent Learning*, Ontario Secondary School Teacher's Federation, 1989

The Role of Analytical and Holistic Evaluation

Most teachers are highly experienced with analytical evaluation. It has an important role to play in the teaching process as it provides students with a knowledge of the criteria being used to evaluate their performance and a clear picture of their areas of strengths and weaknesses. This allows students to focus on individual elements in a concentrated way. However, by concentrating on the parts of the whole rather than the whole itself, analytical evaluation does not give students an indication of the overall impression of their work or their performance.

Holistic evaluation focuses on the overall work or performance. The evaluator awards a single mark or grade based on the overall impression created. For example, if a student were delivering a seminar, the mark or grade would be based on the total effect, not on adding up a series of marks on sub-categories. Many state that holistic evaluation is much closer to the evaluation we do in our everyday life beyond the classroom, where we usually observe something and then sum it up by saying, "That was really great" or "That wasn't very good".

Like analytical evaluation, holistic evaluation needs to be based on articulated criteria. The evaluators have these criteria in mind as they judge the performance. The evaluation is based on how well they feel the students achieved the criteria overall, not on separate categories as with analytical evaluation.

This type of evaluation has been found to be very reliable. Often analytical scoring, which awards a number of marks to each criterion, distorts the evaluation. For example, if five marks are available for evidence or support and the work or performance lacks any support at all, only the five marks may be deducted. With holistic scoring that distortion would not occur. The holistic approach is even more reliable when more than one evaluator is involved. It is usually advisable, then, to have other students evaluate performance, whether it be a presentation or a piece of writing. The more practice students and teachers get in doing this type of evaluation, the more reliable the evaluation becomes. The teacher and students should openly discuss the marks or grades given and the reasons for awarding them. They should then try to reach consensus.

Some jurisdictions have developed procedures that combine holistic and analytical marking. The following Profile Sheet and associated descriptors illustrate one such procedure. It is largely holistic, but it does give students important feedback in specific areas. To help illustrate its usage, two student writing samples are included in this section and are accompanied by completed profile sheets.

The Evaluation Profile

This profile (see page 75) illustrates a set of criteria for evaluating the argumentative essay by combining analytical and holistic elements. Such a profile may be adapted to the summative evaluation of any product. For example, the criteria could be altered to evaluate another genre of writing or a seminar presentation. A blank evaluation profile has been included (see page 94). You may wish to use it with your students and have them work collaboratively to design criteria and a similar evaluation profile for whatever assignment they are working on.

If you are evaluating analytically, you may wish to put the percentage of marks that are available for demonstrating success in each of the criteria areas. Or you may wish to use the profile to score the work holistically. In this case, simply indicate to the student with a check where the strengths and weaknesses are and give a score based on the overall impression created by the piece or the presentation. Used this way, the profile gives good feedback to students without your having to spend time writing lengthy explanations concerning the quality of their effort.

If you are using the profile to grade holistically, you will notice the two major criteria to keep in mind: the quality of the argument and the quality of the writing. More specific analytical feedback can be given by checking the writing in terms of the three sub-criteria for each of the two major categories. The details that describe each of the criterion should be discussed or worked out with the students.

For the quality of the argument

The thesis
> How well is it stated?
> Is it sufficiently clear and focused?

The organization
> How logical is the development of the argument?
> Is it systematic?
> Are minor points subordinated to major points?

Evidence
> Are facts presented in support of the argument?
> Is extraneous evidence omitted?
> Are opinions and assertions supported?

For the quality of the writing

Clarity of expression
> Are sentences complete and comprehensible?
> Is there logical connection between ideas?

Use of standard English
> Is the writing acceptable in an academic context?
> Is it grammatically correct?
> Are spelling and punctuation correct?

Use of stylistic devices
> Has the writing been made more interesting and vivid through the use of metaphor, simile, anecdote, wit, irony, and so on?

SENIOR ENGLISH ARGUMENTATIVE ESSAY
RAPID-IMPRESSION EVALUATION CHECKLIST

EXCEPTIONAL (Meets and exceeds all thinking and writing objectives) 90-100%

The quality of the argument and the quality of expression are outstanding. They are integrated and reinforce each other. The essay presents itself as an impressive unity of all six sub-criteria. The thesis shows complexity of thought, the organization is seamless, and the quality of evidence is convincing. The language, syntax, and use of rhetorical devices all reinforce the meaning, and the overall style adds an element of artistry to the effect.

SUPERIOR (Meets the thinking and writing objectives to a high degree) 80-89%

The quality of the argument and the quality of expression are impressive. Generally, they are integrated and reinforce each other. The essay presents itself as a unity, but there is a sense of lack of strength in one or two of the sub-criteria areas; for example, the thesis might lack sufficient complexity, the supporting evidence might be weak, or mechanical faults might distract the reader at times.

COMPETENT (Meets the thinking and writing objectives to a substantial degree) 70-79%

The quality of the argument and the quality of expression show some complexity but lack the sophistication and integration that mark a superior or outstanding response. The student can take a position, organize his/her thinking, select evidence to support the thesis, and write in such a way that the overall impression is one of control. There are no major weaknesses in any of the sub-criteria that detract seriously from the overall effect.

ADEQUATE (Meets the thinking and writing objectives to an adequate degree) 60-69%

The quality of the argument and the quality of expression are adequate, but the student has not excelled with most of the sub-criteria. The student can sustain and support a straightforward position without obviously contradictory elements and can express it in terms that do not interfere with or detract from the reader's understanding. The structure is likely to adhere closely to a formula (e.g., the five-paragraph essay). Some areas may show weaknesses, but the weaknesses should not interfere with the reader's general understanding.

MARGINALLY ADEQUATE (Meets some of the thinking and writing objectives to some degree) 50-59%

The quality of the argument and/or quality of expression demonstrate serious deficiency in one or more of the sub-criteria areas. Although the reader is able to grasp the writer's basic argument, that argument may be simplistic, poorly organized, and/or poorly supported, or may contain contradictory elements. As well, the response could be seriously weakened by lack of clarity in expression. In fact, if the overall expression is inadequate, this is sufficient to reduce the essay to the unacceptable level. Serious weakness in any one of these areas might be so apparent as to create an overall impression of weakness, and thus reduce the response to the unacceptable level.

INADEQUATE (Meets few, if any, of the thinking and writing objectives) 0-49%

The quality of the argument and/or the quality of expression fail to meet, even minimally, the writing objectives for the argumentative essay. The student is unable either to formulate or to sustain a position and/or cannot write without causing serious reader confusion. Essays that are completely off topic or that deliberately distort the topic also fall into this category.

From *OAC Examination Handbook: English: Language and Literature*, Ontario Ministry of Education, 1991.

EVALUATION PROFILE FOR THE ARGUMENTATIVE ESSAY

Name: _____

Topic: _____

		Inadequate	Marginally Adequate	Adequate	Competent	Superior	Exceptional
Quality of Argument	Thesis	....	....	....	....	....	....
	Organization	....	....	....	....	....	....
	Evidence	....	....	....	....	....	....
	Clarity of Expression	....	....	....	....	....	....
Quality of Writing	Use of Standard English	....	....	....	....	....	....
	Use of Stylistic Devices	....	....	....	....	....	....

General Comments:

From *OAC Examination Handbook: English: Language and Literature*, Ontario Ministry of Education, 1991.

Sample Argumentative Essays

The following two argumentative essays have been evaluated using the Rapid Impression Checklist and the Evaluation Profile for the Argumentative Essay. The essays were written by students under the time constraints of an examination.

Student Response #1

An Exceptional Essay Response
Within the examination context, the following response meets and exceeds all the thinking and writing objectives.

Question
"Good literature is not an escape from reality; it is, in fact, a plunge into a deeper reality where universal truths are glimpsed."

Using the above statement as a focus, assess the extent to which it applies to *two* of the major works studied this term.

Student response
A great deal of modern literature invites the reader to escape from reality by presenting a vision of an unreal reality. Popular genres such as romance, mystery, and even some science fiction invite readers to escape into wish worlds and fantasy worlds and thus often ignore the deeper realities of human existence. But in the circles of fine literature, written by those who wish to probe the human psyche, motives go beyond mere escapism and even aesthetic appreciation, and these works force the reader to explore and contemplate the realm of the deepest realities that the common man does not usually grasp. Such literature invites us into a journey to see what we are and how we work.

This invitation is obvious in *Heart of Darkness* and *A Man for All Seasons*, two works which explore the universal truths that both bless and plague mankind. As good works of literature, they both make excellent use of example and also of literary styles to reinforce these deeper realities and develop them to the point at which we can grasp them with both hands and make ourselves look directly at them. *Heart of Darkness* gives us a glimpse of the darker side of the human spirit, while *A Man for All Seasons* demonstrates the survival of the human spirit over those inner forces of darkness.

The brutal reality of *Heart of Darkness* is inescapable. Marlow's journey into the heart of Africa to find the mysterious Kurtz parallels our own search for self-knowledge, which ultimately includes awareness of the evil in our own hearts. Marlow feels as if he is journeying "to the centre of the world", and, in a way, he is. And so are we.

Kurtz, the object of Marlow's quest, symbolizes the darkness and evil within Marlow, and, since we identify with the questing Marlow, in us all. Kurtz's utterly egotistical view of himself is the basis on which he builds his primitive empire of "unsound motives". He had been representative of the perfect Western enlightened man, with ideas and so much to say; and yet, upon entering the jungle, he had lost his "self", at least his outward, social self. However, what he had found was his true self, the heart of every man, the heart of darkness and evil, a concept that forces us to examine our own sense of self and the corrupting power of egotism.

For us, Marlow completes the view of this evil. Like us, he is the one on the outside looking in, or as he puts it, "peering over the edge of a precipice into a chasm where the sun does not shine." Marlow finds that to survive the primitive voice of the jungle, the heart of darkness, he must control himself, and limit his action. This is the test that Kurtz failed and thereby engendered his fall to his darker self. As Marlow observes, "He had no restraint." Marlow was witness to Kurtz's fall, and, like us, was both fascinated and repulsed by it. Kurtz's final fall (and ironically his ultimate comment of self-knowledge) came about minutes before his death, with the sublime and terrifying admission: "The horror! The horror!" This is the horror of the human soul corrupted when the mind retains all that it ever knew of good, and yet it chooses evil. This "horror" is Kurtz's tragedy. Marlow, the witness, and the person with whom the reader identifies, can only agree, after seeing what such a civilized man had become. Here then is the most brutal of realities, the reality that we ultimately are base beings, totally capable of both spiritual and moral corruption and degradation, regardless of any presumed "enlightenment". The only safeguard appears to be restraint and control, which Marlow manages to display.

The "deeper realities" offered in *A Man for All Seasons* are of a more straightforward nature. It is a story of overcoming the desire for corruption by rejecting it, not by integrating it, as was the case with Morrow in *Heart of Darkness*. Sir

Thomas More is the one man who defies corruption and the temptations of the rewards it offers, namely, life and freedom. More is a devout man of God and of the Catholic Church, and is faced with a test between this loyalty and his loyalty to the King of England. More is persecuted from the time he fails to acknowledge the validity of the King's remarriage to Anne Boleyn, without the annulment he sought from the Pope. His loyalties and his sense of self are tried again and again. He loses his joy, his repute, social stature, and, ultimately, his freedom. Though many people might be persuaded by this to give up that which they believe in, More does not sway, and maintains his ideology, his faith, to the end, even when faced with his own death: "A man's soul is his self." More is a remarkable character; undeniably a great man and we stand in awe of such resolution.

Although the themes here are not so complex as those in *Heart of Darkness*, they run parallel to the choices facing mankind today. In an age where social opportunity and the lure of money and power outweigh everything else for many people, there are few who stand up, take a firm position, regardless of what is thought about them, and stay with it to the end, as bitter as it might be. All of More's colleagues are corrupted easily, and their consciences dangle by their feet, while More's conscience is held as a banner before him. He will not be damned for "not doing according to (his) conscience", and almost cannot stand the fact that everyone does what he is told, regardless of conscience: "Oh Sweet Jesus! These plain, simple men!" However, More is not a simple man, but rather, one that is of the greatest calibre. He is a man who defies his own heart of darkness, and reaches for something higher. Curiously, his reality is often other people's fantasy.

And thus, three journeys into "deeper realities" are complete. One leads to utter darkness and loss of self, another leads to a kind of self-awareness of the heart of darkness, and the third defies the darkness and shines instead. How much is glimpsed and touched upon indeed in these two works. We have explored the deepest realities and the deepest truths, and have come away as deeper people, as happens with all great literature.

From: *OAC Examination Handbook: English: Language and Literature*, Ontario Ministry of Education, 1991.

EVALUATION PROFILE FOR THE ARGUMENTATIVE ESSAY

Name: _Peter Yee_

Topic: _Good literature_

		Inadequate	Marginally Adequate	Adequate	Competent	Superior	Exceptional
Quality of Argument	Thesis						•
	Organization						•
	Evidence						•
Quality of Writing	Clarity of Expression						•
	Use of Standard English						•
	Use of Stylistic Devices						•

General Comments:

An exceptional essay! Your focus on the two key elements of the quotation — "good literature" and "deeper reality" throughout was particularly strong. Your argument was exceptional in a number of ways; for example making a distinction between "popular literature" and "fine literature" at the outset was certainly important, your detailed discussion of the deeper realities faced by the three key characters on their separate journeys was convincing, and your awareness of the differing complexity of themes in the two novels added depth. Strong imagery and complex syntax throughout reinforced your position. Congratulations.

Mark   *100%*

From OAC Examination Handbook: English: Language and Literature, Ontario Ministry of Education, 1991.

Student Response #2

An Adequate Essay Response
The following response meets the thinking and writing objectives to an adequate degree.

Question
"Man is his own worst enemy."

To what extent do you think this statement is true of Lear in *King Lear?*

Student response

In the Shakespearean play, *King Lear*, an excellent example of "Man is his own worst enemy" is King Lear himself, whose pride, ruthlessness, and unforgiving obstinacy bring about his downfall.

In the opening scene we have Lear demanding a verbal statement of love from his three daughters. Two of them, Goneril and Regan, through the use of honied words, win their father's heart and a good portion of his kingdom. The other, Cordelia, whose love is true, receives banishment for speaking the truth. Along with his daughter he banishes the Earl of Kent, whose loyalty to the king is unsurpassed. These actions set off a train of events which will haunt Lear for the remainder of his life.

The two daughters to whom he was kind return their love by driving him from his throne, home, and mind. Lear begins to see his mistake, but it is far too late, for he has already dug his own grave and is soon driven into madness by his own self-tormenting regret. Lear begins an inner conflict with himself when he realizes the source of his sorrow was brought upon him by his own hand. Thus Lear soon loses all — his kingdom, his sanity, and the one daughter who loved him even though he was unkind.

Lear is the ultimate example of self-destruction. He dies poor, wretched, and in total humiliation, and though it is his own kin who actually brought about his tragic death, it can be said that he was his own worst enemy.

From: *OAC Examination Handbook: English: Language and Literature*, Ontario Ministry of Education, 1991.

EVALUATION PROFILE FOR THE ARGUMENTATIVE ESSAY

Name: _Jas Singh_

Topic: _King Lear_

		Inadequate	Marginally Adequate	Adequate	Competent	Superior	Exceptional
Quality of Argument	Thesis				•		
	Organization			•			
	Evidence	•					
	Clarity of Expression		•				
Quality of Writing	Use of Standard English			•			
	Use of Stylistic Devices		•				

General Comments:

While your thesis is competent and a number of elements in your response are also adequate, as you can see from the profile above, the inadequate development of your position and lack of supporting evidence leave the reader with the overall impression that the response is only marginally adequate. If you had carried through on the development of the three points of your thesis, your mark would have certainly been higher. As well, make sure your stylistic devices assist rather than hinder your meaning. For example, is the reader to take it literally that Lear has "already dug his own grave"? I see lots of potential here; it will just take more time and effort on your part.

Mark 55%

From: *OAC Examination Handbook: English: Language and Literature,* Ontario Ministry of Education, 1991.

CHAPTER SIX

Collaborative Evaluation — The Process of Moderation

The term "moderation" is used to refer to a collaborative process by which an individual teacher's evaluation is given wider validity by a team of markers. The process, which is consistent with the principles of assessment and evaluation, has several advantages. For the public, moderation ensures that common standards are maintained and honored. For the teacher, moderation leaves evaluation essentially in his/her hands, and establishes a collaborative framework in which evaluation and other issues can be discussed. It can generate excellent opportunities for professional development. It leads us to think about what we value, and allows us to share those values with others. For the learner, moderation provides a set of appropriate models and a clearer understanding of the criteria used for evaluation.

When moderation is initiated, a healthy process is set in motion among teachers, learners, and the community. The process is self-correcting and self-perpetuating, and is based on authentic interaction and discourse. The ultimate goal is self-evaluation by learners and teachers.

Using the Process of Moderation

Each department or school should develop a program congenial to its own needs, structures, and interests. However, the following key principles should underlie all programs.

1. Moderation must evolve slowly as teachers, students, and the wider community interact and learn from one another.

2. The process is inductive, beginning with students' real work (written or oral) and teachers' real responses to such work.

3. Portfolios that include a range of samples and a selection of the students' best written and oral work are the most valid indicators of student performance.

4. From the portfolios, pieces of authentic writing or oral work representing all relevant ranges and levels are collected. Teachers discuss what they consider to be the best and worst of all the pieces, and articulate the criteria that place these pieces in the various categories. Finally, the team selects samples or "benchmarks" with criteria representing the complete range.

5. The process is essentially collaborative: teachers collaborate with teachers, with students, and with curriculum planners.

How to Get Started on the Process of Moderation

A program of moderation can begin on a small scale. All it takes is a team of three or four teachers who decide to collaborate in their evaluation of student writing or oral language.

1. Each brings to the meeting a set of oral or written compositions drawn from regular course assignments. These should include pieces representing a range in quality. There may or may not be some agreement in advance as to the nature of the assignments.

2. The teachers then mark the entire set of papers holistically. The purpose of this initial holistic response is to generate discussion, and bring to light the implicit values governing their intuitive responses.

3. After all the work has been graded holistically, they then discuss the discrepant grades. The purpose is not to push for agreement, but to formulate some rationale for each evaluation.

4. The papers or tapes that elicited agreement can then be probed

for criteria that might justify the grade. Again, the goal is to make such criteria explicit. What is usually most surprising is the broad range of agreement and the strength of agreed-upon standards.

5. There may be interesting, lively discussions about teaching, learning, and curriculum. Often such discussions lead teachers to re-examine curriculum and instruction.

6. It will probably take three or four sessions before criteria and benchmarks can be clearly stated, as the teachers become more confident about shared standards and more aware of their own biases.

7. At this point, there may be sufficient agreement to settle on samples or benchmarks that reveal specific criteria.

8. The next step in the process is to involve students in discussing why these samples illustrate benchmarks. Perhaps the students can go through the same holistic marking process, and then articulate their own criteria. Here, too, discrepancies can be the subject of very fruitful discussion. Whatever the nature of the discussion, teachers will find the students' responses useful. Such discussion will provide insight for the students, as well as for the teachers as they continue to formulate and modify evaluative criteria. Enlightened by this new perspective, teachers can return to their colleagues with fresh ideas.

Although moderation in this form could spread widely through jurisdictions, it might also stay on a small scale within a department or school. Whatever happens, the process should be a positive one that ensures that other external assessment remains secondary to and in the service of the curricular goals and instructional practices of the interaction of the teacher, learner, and community. At the same time, it can establish real standards of achievement that are understood and agreed upon by all.

Conclusion

The accelerating pace of change in society is affecting both teaching strategies and the use of resources. Curricula are changing, and although assessment and evaluation methods have not kept pace, thoughtful teachers and administrators are recognizing that evaluation approaches must also be amended. There is increasing recognition that assessment and evaluation should focus on positive achievement and the development of processes of learning. Students are making commitments to their own learning and are being involved in the collaborative design of assessment and evaluation approaches and instruments. In schools where effective evaluation is in place, students are actively engaged in many practices such as:

- using learning logs, where students record in writing or on audio- or videotape what they have learned, and what they may still be puzzled about;
- composing problems, assignments, and questions instead of always responding to those of others;
- demonstrating or applying their knowledge in examination situations rather than regurgitating their notes and those of others;
- completing or suggesting alternative possibilities for stories, descriptions, and events;
- engaging with authentic texts and dramatizing stories and events;
- using checklists and similar devices to record and track achievement;

- recognizing the seriousness and validity of self- and peer-assessment;
- maintaining achievement profiles with benchmark samples of their work;
- recognizing that marks are very often arbitrary and subjective and no substitute for the examination of authentic materials, performances, or applications.

Assessment and evaluation strategies that direct curricula and practices like these also reflect curricula that are interactive, positive, and student-centered. There is high public interest in accountability, and there are many people outside the classroom who want to evaluate what happens there. It is important for teachers, therefore, to be proactive and use approaches such as the process of moderation to explain how and why they evaluate as they do.

Phasing in Peer- and Self-Assessment and Evaluation

A self-directed learner is one who can assess and evaluate his/her own progress and achievement. If students are not experienced, begin with anecdotal, nonthreatening evaluation designed to help students help one another to improve or focus more on what they are doing. Get them used to the idea that evaluation is a learning as well as a measuring device that is not always designed to end up as a "mark." In fact, having students give themselves and one another a mark before they are used to evaluation as a learning activity may be very counterproductive. Here are some suggestions for phasing in evaluation as a learning strategy.

Step 1: Diagnostic and Formative Peer- and Self-Evaluation

Have students become accustomed to self- and peer-evaluation. Ask them to diagnose their own and other's needs to assist progress during the formative stages of learning. For example, at various points ask students to take stock of where they are and what they need to do in order to reach their goal. Such formative evaluation may be accomplished through the use of anecdotal comments (written and/or oral) or checklists that identify areas for improvement and provide helpful suggestions. You might find it beneficial to start with group peer- and group self-evaluation before moving to individual peer- and self-evaluation.

Have students establish the habit of determining and applying specific criteria when they are evaluating their own and others' progress and/or achievement. Students must have an objective framework for their responses to their own and others' efforts.

Step 2: From Formative to Summative Evaluation

When students are comfortable applying criteria, you may wish to translate some checklists or anecdotal comments into a letter grade or a mark.

You may award a grade for:

- completion of a specified number of peer-evaluations (this is an important way to encourage students to help one another in the various phases of the writing process);
- completion of a specified number of self-evaluations;
- ability to apply criteria, for example, a student's ability to apply certain editorial criteria to another student's writing and/or to his/her own writing.

Step 3: Marking One Another

Once students have been evaluated for their ability to evaluate and they have reached a certain level of competence, you can start having them apply a mark or a grade to the work of other students and to themselves when summative evaluation is required.

At this stage, stress a collegial evaluation atmosphere. Students will be more comfortable having more than one evaluator assess their efforts and come to some consensus about the grade to be awarded.

In fact, the situation becomes an important learning experience. An individual group's mark or an individual student's mark is more likely to be accepted (and is perhaps more accurate) when it is the result of consensus of teacher, self, and peer marks, the proportional values determined by the degree of evaluation expertise on the part of the various evaluators.

While this final stage could conceivably happen with younger students, it is more likely to be reached with senior students. By senior high school, students should be adept at setting learning objectives, selecting learning strategies, and establishing criteria to evaluate their own and others' success with those objectives, both formatively and summatively. In this way, evaluation becomes "built in" and students will truly have become self-directed, independent learners.

Establishing Criteria

If students are to be involved in peer- and self-evaluation, they must also be involved in establishing the criteria they will use. You should discuss with them, and have them discuss in groups, what criteria such as the following mean in practice:

- leads discussion
- develops an argument
- explains
- persuades
- describes
- instructs/directs
- challenges
- justifies
- questions
- modifies viewpoint, suggests alternatives
- analyzes
- predicts outcomes
- solves a problem
- prioritizes
- makes a decision
- modifies language in response
- listens attentively to audience
- summarizes
- redirects group focus
- draws in other group members

A SAMPLE CHECKLIST USING SELECTED CRITERIA
FOR OBSERVING INDIVIDUALS IN GROUP WORK

Some of the criteria listed on previous pages could be used to record observations of individual activity in a group on a number of occasions. Students should be involved in establishing criteria to be selected. Different criteria could be used for each student.

Purpose: _____

Members: _____

Student(s) Observed: _____

Achievement:

U = unsatisfactory
W = weak
S = satisfactory
E = excellent

Criteria	Achieve- ment	Dates	Observer
1. a. _____			
b. _____			
2. a. _____			
b. _____			
3. a. _____			
b. _____			
4. a. _____			
b. _____			
5. a. _____			
b. _____			

Comments

A Student's Guide for Interpreting Questions

Generally, a question has three parts: a key verb that tells you what you are supposed to do, an object that tells you on what you are to perform the task, and a limited factor or factors that tell(s) you how to go about it. Here is an example.

Explain the methods used to create humor in *Danny the Champion of the World* by referring to events at the climax of the story.

Key verb: explain

Object: methods used to create humor

Limiting factor: refers to a specific part of the story – events at the climax. Notice how the question defines your response. It would do you no good to refer to a part of the story other than the climax. So, before beginning your answer, make sure that you read the question carefully and don't do more or less than it tells you to do.

The Key Verb

The verb is the most important part of the question since it tells you what you must do. The following is a list of various verbs you will find in typical questions. Beside each is an explanation of its meaning and a suggestion concerning the length of response required. One of the best ways to learn what each requires is to try making up questions using the verbs. Discuss these with a partner, in a group, or in a whole-class discussion.

State: be as clear and concise as possible in answering

Explain: go into detail and use a step-by-step method

Evaluate: give your opinion about the worth of something, based on evidence

Point out: look specifically at some aspect; be precise

Summarize: look at the whole work or concept and reduce it to its main ideas

Describe: tell about something; go into some detail about it

Illustrate: go directly to the work in question, and by means of short, key quotations and/or specific references come up with support for a point. Unless you are writing an essay, do not use lengthy quotations. Often a word or a sentence is sufficient to illustrate a point. If a question has two key verbs, for example: "Describe and illustrate. . ." remember to do both.

List: (without a modifying expression, such as "in order") jot down at random

Trace: arrange items in a meaningful sequence, such as cause and effect relationship, chronological order, or order of importance

Outline: sketch a plan, perhaps with headings and subheadings, that could be developed or filled in later

Define: explain the meaning of a particular expression. A definition should be illustrated with at least one specific example (e.g., demote — to reduce in rank)

Compare: look at two things or ideas, and call attention to similarities and differences. Comparison usually requires specific examples.

Contrast: much the same as compare, except that it focuses on the differences between items rather than on the similarities. It, too, requires specific examples.

Analyze: break down into parts and examine each part critically.

To analyze a character, you might consider two or three important personality traits. Give concrete examples to illustrate each trait and then show the relationship between actions and personalities.

Discuss: formulate an idea or thesis about something, and then substantiate that thesis with examples. You are usually expected to go into some detail in your answer. Because it is so ambiguous, this term is best avoided, particularly in examination questions.

Evaluation Profile

EVALUATION PROFILE

Name: _____

Topic: _____

	Inadequate	Marginally Adequate	Adequate	Competent	Superior	Exceptional

General Comments:

Adapted from OAC Examination Handbook: English: Language and Literature, Ontario Ministry of Education, 1991.

Bibliography

Bruner, J. *Actual Minds, Possible Worlds.* Cambridge, MA: Harvard University Press, 1986.

Clarke, J., R. Wideman & S. Eadie. *Together We Learn.* Scarborough, ON: Prentice Hall Canada, Inc., 1990.

Goodman, K., Y. Goodman & W. Hood. *The Whole Language Evaluation Book.* Portsmouth, NH: Heinemann Educational Books Inc., 1989.

Graham, N. *Exploring Perspectives.* Whitby, ON: McGraw Hill-Ryerson Ltd., 1991.

Hillocks, G. Jr. "What Works in Teaching Composition: A Meta-Analysis of Experimental Treatment Studies." *American Journal of Education,* Dec. 1984.

Metropolitan Toronto School Board. *Linking Evaluation with Learning.* Toronto, ON: Metropolitan Toronto School Board, 1989.

Ontario Ministry of Education. *Basic English OAIP: Assessment Strategies and Materials.* Toronto, ON: Queen's Printer, 1990.

_____. *OAC Examination Handbook: English: Language and Literature,* Toronto, ON: Queen's Printer, 1991.

_____. *Senior English OAIP: Assessing Writing,* Toronto, ON: Queen's Printer, 1992.

_____. *Senior English OAIP: Promoting Learning through Assessment.* Toronto, ON: Queen's Printer, 1992.

_____. *Student Evaluation in English*. Toronto, ON: Queen's Printer, 1987.

Ontario Secondary School Teachers' Federation. *Independent Learning: Process to Product*. Toronto, ON: The Professional Development Committee, 1989.

Probst, R. *Response and Analysis: Teaching Literature in Junior and Senior High School*. Portsmouth, NH: Heinemann Educational Books Inc., 1988.

Smith, F. *Insult to Intelligence*. New York: NY: Arbor House, 1986.

White, M. *Teaching and Assessing Writing*. San Francisco, CA: Jossey-Bass Publishers, Inc., 1988.